Africans:
People of Color
in Pre-Islamic &
Islamic History

Africans: People of Color in Pre-Islamic & Islamic History

Amir N. Muhammad

Contents

Acknowledgments

I would like to give thanks to Allah (the Creator of the heavens and the earth; all that is between them; and of all what we see and of all that we don't) for His mercy and kindness, and for the knowledge and opportunities He has blessed me with in this life.

I would like to thank my wife, D. Habeebah Muhammad for her undaunted support and encouragement and for the long hours she devoted in editing this as well as my other books, and yet, never for a while, neglecting her duties towards her family as a righteous Muslim, a loving wife, a caring mother, a good friend and a great business woman. Her herbal skin care products are sold in many places around the country, and she still works a 9-5. Go girl! Behind every successful man there is a good woman, Amen.

I dedicate this book to my youngest daughter, Aisha J. Muhammad who someday may become that next Professor of History and a Linguist who will help in furthering the research of Islamic history and its connections in the development of the Americas and the Caribbean.

Introduction

With the name of Allah, Most Gracious, Most Merciful.

The German scholar Herbert Wendt points to the fact that Asia was the cradle of the black race in his book *It Began in Babel*. Our intention in this book is to highlight and bring into focus the rich and long history of the African and Muslims of African heritage known throughout time by many names from the children of Ham to, Kushites, Abyssinians, Zengh, Hargities, Nubians, Zanj, Beja, Moors, Negro, to Black. Within this book you will find dating back to 776 AD an African man who was a Muslim, whose full name was Abu Uthman amr bin Bahr al Fukaymi Al-Basri Al-Jahiz, better known as Al-Jahiz. Al-Jahiz wrote many books, and in one of his books he addresses the race problem more than 1,200 years ago. Al-Jahiz also highlights some of the common qualities and good nature of the black man, which still exists in him today. He points out that blacks are very generous, they have a natural gift for rhythmic dancing, are the best singers, they express themselves in a lively manner, physically stronger, they are always happy, smiling, and optimistic. Al-Jahiz dispels the false notion that blacks could not read, think, or write.

Africans: People of Color in Pre-Islamic and Islamic History highlights some of the better known Africans before Prophet Muhammad's (*saw*) time, such as Luqman, Aesop, Hannibal, the Queen of Sheba, Antar, and others. At least eleven known men and women of African descent were among Prophet Muhammad's (*saw*) companions during his time. Prophet Muhammad (*saw*) could trace his family to African Hamitic and Semitic heritage.

In Islamic history, in 615 AD Africa was the first place where Muslims made hijra (flight) and sought refuge. They took shelter with the king of Abyssinia and it was in Africa that the first Muslim community grew outside of the Arabian area. After the migration of the Prophet (*saw*) to Medina more than seventy Abyssinian converts came to Medina. The next time Islam came into Africa was in 640 AD when General Amru captured Egypt. In 642 Alexandria surrendered. From Egypt, Islamic influence extended in three directions, through the Red Sea to the eastern coastal areas, up the Nile valley to the Sudan, and across the western desert. The conquest of North Africa was completed in 708 AD when Musa Ibn Nusair subdued Morocco. By 711AD the Muslim Berbers and other tribes from North Africa went into Spain and began conquering it. They became known as the Moors. By 725 AD the Muslims of the second wave came from West Africa, from the Mali and Senegal regions. They became the rulers of Spain leading in the arts, education, the sciences, navigation, agriculture, and civilization.

We find in history that the first civilized Europeans were the Greeks, who were chiefly civilized by the Africans (Phoenicians) of the Nile Valley. The Greeks transmitted this culture to the Romans, who eventually lost it, bringing on a dark age for five hundred years. Civilization was restored to Europe when another group of Africans, the Moors, brought this dark age to an end, meanwhile recivilizing the Christian barbarians of Europe. The Europeans learned how to cultivate such crops as cotton, rice, silk, oranges, sugar, and lemons from Muslims. The Moors were experts in music, well cultured in dress, manners and etiquette. Three of the best known world travelers, historians, and explorers were men of African heritage, two of them were Muslims, and the other was of Islamic heritage.

This book points out some great African Muslim scholars, military leaders, and religious leaders such as Tarik Bin Ziyad, Ibrahim Al-Mahdi, Kafur Al-Ikshidi, 'Abd Allah ibn Yasin, Yusuf Ibn Tashfin, Askia the Great, Mansa Musa, Ahmad Baba, Uthman (Usman) dan-Fodio, and others. The book also highlights some of the better known Muslim slave holders and traders such as Tippu Tib and Muhammad Bello.

History shows that the spread of Islam came into Africa in many different ways and forms and with the different Islamic schools of law based on the various regions. In West Africa Islam came by the way of North Africa, as well as with a few native West Africans. The Muslims of West Africa followed the Maliki school of law, and in East Africa, Islam came to them from the Arabian peninsula, by the way of the Arabian Sea, and they followed the Shafi's school of law.

To my Pan-African brothers and sisters, the history of the majority of the people of African heritage that were part of the African Diaspora during the slavery period in the United States, South America, and the Caribbean came from West Africa, and the remaining 10% or so were from North Africa. The majority of us are not from Egypt, nor East Africa. Our most current African history and connections are mainly from West Africa. Therefore when scholars and other people leave out our West African heritage. They leave our genetic connections, history, and contributions. They are doing a great disservice to us as a people. They are leaving us disconnected from our past and genetic link, leaving us to be dysfunctional.

West Africa had many great cities and city states like Timbuktu, Djenne, Darfur, Walata, Gao, Sao, and Agades; and some great empires such as Ghana, Mali, Songhay, Kanem, Bornu, and Ashanti.

In 1010 AD the king of Ghana Za Kasi accepted and converted to Islam. According to Rudolph Windsor in his book *From Babylon to Timbuktu* he states that the King's conversion was not by force, but he was persuaded to convert to Islam by the merchants of the city of Gao. By 1240 AD Mandingo merchants played a great part in the transportation of Islam to their people and empire.

G-d willing, you will find among the many great men and women of color and African heritage in the following pages something you may learn from, and perhaps gain some insight and encouragement.

People of Color (Africans and Arabs)
from a Biblical Heritage

Prophet Idris (Enoch) was a son of Cain and grandson of Adam. He is referred to in the Holy Qur'an as a man of constancy and steadfastness. In Prophet Idris' (Enoch) 4th generation his great grandson was Prophet Noah. From Noah's children came the Semitic, Hamitic, and the Japhitic tribes and people. In this work we will focus on the Semitic and Hamitic people.

Idris was the first person in the world to learn how to write. The knowledge of arithmetic and astronomy began with him. Idris (Enoch) was the father of Methuselah; Methuselah was the father of Lamech; Lamech was the father of Noah.

Lamech had two wives one named Adah and the other named Zillah. Adah gave birth to Jabal. Jabal was the father of those who dwell in tents and have cattle. *Genesis 4:19-20.* His brother's name was Jubal. He was the father of all those who play the lyre and pipe. *Genesis 4: 21.*

Zillah was the mother of Turbal-Cain and his sister Na'amah. Turbal-cain was the forger of all instruments of bronze and iron. *Genesis 4:22.*

The Children of Noah's son Shem:
The Beginning of the Arabs in the Bible

Noah's oldest son's name was Shem. The sons of Shem were Elam, Asshur, Arpach'shad, Lud, and Aram. The sons of Aram were Uz,

Hul, Gether, and Mash. The son of Arpach'shad was Shelah, who had a son named Eber. Eber was Shem's great grandson. Eber was the father of two sons Peleg (*Adnan*) and Joktan (*Qahtan*).

From Eber's son Peleg's (*Adnan*) children came the ancestry of Abraham, Isaac, Jacob, Ismail and the descendants of the northern Arabian tribes called "*Al-Arab Al-Musta'ribah*" (The Arabized Arabs). Some of the descendants from these tribes are the Kinanah, Al-Nasr, Malik, and Fihr (*Quraysh*).

Peleg (*Adnan*) at the age of thirty gave birth to a son named Re'u. Re'u was the father of Serug, who became the father of Nahor. Nahor was the father of Terah. Terah of Ur had three children Abram, Nahor, and Haran. Haran was the father of Lot.

From Peleg's (*Adnan*) son Ma'ad came Nizar. From Nizar's son Anmar came the descendants of the Quraysh Arabs. Fihr is one of the ancestors of the Quraysh Arabs whose descendants were ancestors of Prophet Muhammad's *(saw)* family on his father side.

From Eber's son Joktan (*Qahtan*) came several southern Arabian tribes, the Almodad, Sheleph, Hazarma,'veth, Jerah, Hador'am, Uzal, Diklah, Obal, Abim'ael, Sheba, Ophir, Hav'ilah, and Jobab. "*Genesis 10: 21-29*".

The parts of the earth inhabited by the children of Shem were parts of Assyria and Elam (Persia) east of the Tigris River, the eastern part of Syria, and parts of the Arabian peninsula.

The people of Ad were named after Adnan (Peleg), the great great grandson of Shem, a son of Noah. Their prophet was Hud and their capital was in Iram, in present day Yemen.

Africa gets its name from the descendants of Joktan (Qahtan). Ophren (Apher) and Japhran led a military expedition against North Africa and Libya, they captured it. When his grandchildren colonized the place, they called it by his name Apher.

The Arabic name for some of the tribes of Qahtan are Abil, Ad, Imlik, Jadis, Jurhum, Tasm, Thamud, Umaiyim, Ya'rub, Saba, Himyar, and Wabir. They are known as the "*Al-Arab Al-Aribah*" (The Arabizing Arabs).

The Children of Noah's Second Son Ham

The curse of G-d was not on Ham and his descendants, as so many believe. First, the Holy Qur'an points to a son of Noah who did not obey his father to board on to the boat at the time of the flood. This son's family was cursed when he ran to a mountain for refuge and drowned in the flood. Secondly, the Bible says, "When Noah awoke from his wine and knew what his youngest son had done to him, he said cursed be Canaan." *Genesis 9:24-25.*

The Bible does not say it was Ham, it speaks of the son of Ham, Canaan. Thirdly, the Bible say's the youngest son did not obey his father. Ham was the second son of Noah, Japheth was the youngest son. According to world opinion the children Ham were black and the children of Shem was brown, and the children of Japheth white. Ham, Shem, and Japheth were brothers. They were all black with Shem, Ham, and Japheth's side coming out lighter due to the difference in climate and the environment, along with intermarriage among the different families and tribes.

In the Bible, it states that the Nephilim were on the earth in the days of Noah and afterward when the sons of G-d came into the daughters of men (Nephilim), and they bore children for them. They were mighty men who were of old age and men of renown. *Genesis 4: 3-4.*

Ham's children were Cush (Ethiopian), Mizriam (Egypt), Phut (Put), and Canaan. Ham's oldest son was Cush. The sons of Cush were Nimrod, Seba, Hav'ilah, Sabtah, Ra'amah, and Sabteca. "*Genesis 10: 8-12*".

Nimrod, the son of Cush ruled Babel, Erech, Accad (Akkad), and Calneh, in the land of Shinar (Babylon), Mesopotamia, and Yemen. Nimrod also ruled Assyria and built the cities of Nineveh, Rehoboth-Ir, Calah, and Resen.

The sons of Cush's son, Ra'amah were Sheba and Dedan. The descendants of Ra'amah lived in southeast Arabia, and the descendants of Hav'ilah lived in southwest Arabia, which today is Yemen. They were known as Cushities, Akkadians, Babylonians, Assyrians, Sumerians, Ethiopians, Abyssinians, and Nubians. Cush was the patriarch of all the Ethiopian tribes in Babylon, Arabia, India and on the Nile River.

The Children of Ham's Second Son

Ham's second son Mizriam (Egypt) was the father of Ludim, An'amim, Leha'bim, Naphtu'him, Pathru'sim, Caslu'hims were known as the Philistines and Caphtorim. All of Mizriam's children lived in Egypt except the Caphtorim and some Philistines. They inhabited the Island of Crete in the Mediterranean Sea.

It's reported that these black Philistines inhabited the land of Canaan and settled along the southern coast of Palestine.

The land of Palestine gets its name from the Philistines who lived in the region.

Pathrusim's descendants were the Egyptians who ruled and lived in (Pathros) Upper Egypt. Mizriam's other children ruled lower Egypt and other parts of North and East Africa. The Lehabim and Ludim occupied the territory west of Egypt now called Libya, and westward. They became known as An'amim, Egyptians, Lehabim, Naphtu'him, Nubians, Philistines (Palestine), Caphtorims, Lubimians, and later Libyans. The Hamitic Egyptians were proficient in mathematics, medicine, engineering, and agriculture.

The Children of Ham's Third Son Phut

The Sons of Put (Phut), Ham's third son's descendants inhabited Somali land. They moved westward into Senegal, and below the Sahara Desert. They used the names Futa, Foul, Fulas, Poul, Poulbe, and Fulbe. They lived in Futa-Torro near Senegal, Futa-Jallon and Futa-Bondu to the north of Sierra Leone. They also lived in Futa-Kasson, Futa-Zora, Futa-Ferlo and Futa-Dugu.

The Children of Ham's Fourth Son Canaan

The Sons of Canaan, Ham's youngest son were Sidon and Heth. The descendants of Canaan became known as Canaanites, Sidonians (Phoenicians), Hittites, Jebusites, Amorites, Gir'gashites, Hivites, Arkites, Zem'arites, Hamathites, Sinites, Sebaites (Sabians), Amorites, Philistines, and Caphtories.

Hittites are descendants of Heth, the grandson of Ham, the son of Canaan. *Genesis 10:15.*

The children of Canaan inhabited territory from Sidon, in the direction of Gerar, as far as Gaza, and in the direction of Sodom, Gomor'rah, Admah, Zeboi'im, and Lasha. The greatest cultural and commercial cities of the black Hamitic-Canaanite were Tyre and Sidon (Zidon). The Phoenicians established a colony in north Africa called Carthage. It was not until the Israelites under Joshua Ben Nun invaded the land of Canaan, that many of the Hamitic-Canaanite tribes migrated to north Africa.

The Greeks called the Sidonians "Phoenicians," the name meaning land of palm. The land of Sidonians was located to the north of Palestine, along the coast of the Mediterranean Sea; bounded by the sea on the west, and by the mountain ranges of Lebanon on the east. The cities of Tyre and Sidon were founded about 2300 BC by Black Phoenicians.

The Phoenician people were proficient in philosophy, astronomy, geometry, arithmetic, and navigation. The Phoenicians also had a powerful Navy. They were skilled in metal work, needle work, and embroidery. They invented the dye known as Tyrian purple. The Phoenicians spoke a Hamitic-Semitic language. The Greeks adopted the Phoenician alphabet.

The holy city of Jerusalem got its name from the Jebusites who were black people and descendants of Canaan. They built and inhabited the city of Jebus, which was the original name of Jerusalem.

Abraham's Family Line with Hagar and Keturah

Abraham's eldest son was Ismail (Ishmael), whose mother was Hagar, a Cushite (Ethiopian). Some of their descendants were known as Hagrites, who were descendants of Cush. Ismail became the father of some Arabs, whose descendants came from Noah's sons Shem and Ham.

Ismail had twelve sons Nebaioth, Kedar, Adbeel, Mibsam, Mishma, Dumah, Massa, Hadad, Tema, Jetur, Naphish, and Kedemah. *Genesis 25:12-16.* Prophet Muhammad *(saw)* was a direct descendant of Ismail. Hashimites are descendants of Hashim. The name has its origin in the descendants of Noah's sons Ham and Shem, descendants marrying together. Examples of such unions are Abraham and Hagar, and Abraham and Keturah. With both couples you have Semitic and Hamitic descendants coming together.

Ismail's descendants dwelt from Hav'ilah unto Shur just before Egypt, and toward Assyria. *Genesis 25:18*. Ismail's son Dumah (*Aduma* in Arabic) lived among the caravans of the De'danites in the land of Tema. The Dedanities were descendants of Cush, son Dedan, and of the descendants of Abraham and Keturah's son Jokshan.

Hadad was the eighth son of Ismail and a King of Edom. Edom was also known as Mount Seir and Idumaea. Tema (*Adumatu* in Arabic) was the twelfth son of Ismail, who inhabited the place named Teman in Edom.

Ismail and Isaac buried their father Abraham in a cave on the land of Ephron (Hebron). Ephron was the son of Zohar the Hittite. *Genesis 25:10* Hittites are descendants of Heth, the grandson of Ham, the son of Canaan. *Genesis 10:15*.

Jaziz, the Hagrite was over the flocks of King David. (*1 Chron. 27:30*). He was a descendant of Hagar.

The Descendants of Abraham and Keturah

Keturah was Abraham's second wife after Sarah died. She was of African heritage. Together they had six sons, Zimran, Jokshan, Medan, Mid'ian, Isbak, and Shuah.

Zimran was Abraham and Keturah's oldest son. Jokshan was the second son of Abraham and Keturah. Jokshan was the father of Sheba and Dedan. The sons of Dedan were Asshu'rim, Letu'shim, and Leummim. There are two cities named after them, Sheba (Saba) was the southern terminus, and Dedan was a major emporium located in the oasis of El-Ula in the northern Hejaz area of Arabia. They both were important centers for the incense trade.

Medan was the third son of Abraham and Keturah. His descendants helped populate the land of Midian.

Mid'ian was the fourth son of Abraham and Keturah. The descendants of Mid'ian were known as Midianites. The sons of

Mid'ian were Ephah, Epher, Hanoch, Abi'da, and Elda'ah. Moses married a Midianite woman.

Ishbak was the fifth son of Abraham and Keturah, and from him came one of the Arabian tribes. Ishbak (Yasbuq) and Shuah (Suhu) are two closely related regions in the steppe region of northern Syria. The Ishbak and Shuah were the northernmost Arab tribes involved in the incense trade.

Shuah was the sixth son of Abraham and Keturah.

Prophet Shu'ayb [Jethro](sa) was a Prophet of Allah and the Priest of Midian. He was the great grandson of Mid'ian. Mid'ian was a son of Abraham by his second wife Keturah. Their descendants became known as Midianites. Shu'ayb (Jethro) was the father-in-law of Prophet Moses (sa). Moses married Zippora'ah, a Midianitie. Together they had at least two sons, one named Gershom and the other Elie'zer.

"It was Mid'ianite traders who passed by and drew Joseph up out of the well pit, and sold him to the Ish'maelites, who took him to Egypt." *Genesis 37:28.* They lived in north western Arabia along the east coast of the Gulf of Aqaba. The sons of Midian, Ephah and Epher are mentioned in eighth-century Assyrian inscriptions as Haiappa and Apparu, and they have been identified with the towns Ghwafah and Ofr. Abi'da has been linked with the tribe Ibadidi, regularly associated with the Thamud. Mid'ian's son Elda'ah is an Arab royal name in Assyrian and Sabean inscriptions.

Pre Islamic African Leaders and Heroes

Cushan-rishathaim a Kushite ruler around (3000 BCE.) was a king of Mesopotamia. The Kushite empire was based in present day Iraq, and stretched from Egypt to present-day Khartoum, and the Mediterranean.

Imhotep (2980 BC) was the real Father of Medicine. He was known as the "Prince of Peace." It's reported that he was the first figure of a physician to stand out clearly in antiquity. Imhotep lived at the court of King Zoser of the third dynasty. Imhotep's father was an architect named Kanofer and his mother's name was Khreduonkh. His wife's name was Ronfrenofert. Imhotep was known as a sage, scribe, chief lector priest, architect, astronomer, poet, proverb-maker, and philosopher. One of his best known sayings is "*Eat, drink, and be merry for tomorrow we shall die.*"

Hatshepsut (1500 BC) of Egypt is known as the greatest female ruler of all time, according to some Egyptologists. Her father Thotmes entrusted her with the management of the kingdom and made her co-ruler. Hatshepsut had several rivals, primarily her two half brothers on her father's side. Hatshepsut's grandmother was Nefertari-Aahmes, an Ethiopian.

Candace was a queen of the Ethiopians. Her servant was taught the truth concerning Jesus the Christ.

Amenophis IV (1350 BC) was better known as Akhenaton, "The First Messiah." His father's name was Amenophis and his mother's name was Tiyi. Both were full blooded Africans. His wife was Nefertiti another full blooded African. Akhenaton preached the gospel of peace and preached it so consistently that when subject nations rebelled he refused to attack them. Centuries before King David wrote the psalms, Akhenaton wrote beautiful psalms of peace. Thirteen hundred years before Jesus the Christ *(sa)* and two thousand years before Prophet Muhammad *(saw)* Akhenaton preached monotheism and lived a gospel of perfect love, brotherhood, truth, and the doctrine of the One G-d. He also taught about the unity that runs through all living things. He taught that G-d was unseen and yet an ever-present compassionate G-d, even toward the chickens. He taught that the father of mankind was made manifest in sunshine, the Creator of the universe and the giver of all good. Akhenaton was also the richest man on earth during his life time.

Nefertiti was a queen of ancient Egypt from (1353-1336 BC). Nefertiti was one of the most powerful women in the history of Egypt. She was the chief wife of the pharaoh Akhenaton. She had six daughters with Akhenaton. She was a worshiper of the Aton (The Sun G-d).

Luqman (1100 BC) was an Ethiopian with wooly hair and a son of Baura. Baura was a son of the sister of Job. Luqman was the first great fabulist. He was also known as the wisest man of the ancient east. There is a Chapter in the Holy Qur'an, Surah 31 which is named after Luqman.

Queen of Sheba (960 BC) was known as Balkis. She was the ruler of Yemen and the mother of King Soloman's son Menelik, the King of Ethiopia.

Aesop (560 BC). The influence of Aesop on western thought and morals is profound. We are all aware of Aesop's fables. Plato, Socrates, Aristophanes, Aristotle, Solon, Cicero, Julius Caesar, Caxton, Shakespeare, La Fontaine, and other great thinkers found inspiration in his words of wisdom. Aesop was a native of Phrygia, in Asia Minor. He was a black man with a flat nose, and large lips.

Hannibal (247-183 BC) of Carthage was born in 247 BC His father was Hamilcar Barca. The Carthaginians were descendants of the Phoenicians who were black people and great merchants. Hannibal has the reputation of being the greatest military leader and strategist of all time. He crossed the Alps with Elephants, and ruled southern Italy for more than fifteen years. His tactics are still taught in leading military academics.

His strategy at Cannae was successfully imitated by Hitler in his attack on Belgium.

Cleopatra II (69-30 BC) was a Queen of Egypt. With her beauty, learning, and culture she fascinated and held two successive masters of the Roman world, first Julius Caesar and the second was Caesar's friend and successor, Mark Antony. Cleopatra was the last ruler of the Macedonian dynasty of the Ptolemies. She became queen in 51 BC at the age of eighteen when her father died. It is reported that Cleopatra spoke Greek, Egyptian, Latin, Ethiopian, Hebrew, Arabic, and Syrian fluently. She had a sister who was named Arsinoe, the Queen of Syria.

Abrah (Abraha) Al-Arsham was the Christian viceroy for the Negus of Abyssinia. Abrahah ruled Yemen in the middle of the 6th century. In 570 AD he undertook a campaign against the north Arabians and marched against Mecca. That campaign became known as the "Year of the Elephant." In a few short years his rule was defeated by the Persians and Abrah was killed by a general named Wahiz.

Abd al-Muttalib ibn Hashim, (b.495-578 AD) was the grand-father of Prophet Muhammad (*saw*). He was also the head of the Banu Hashim clan of the Quraysh tribe. His real name was Shaybah and his mother was Salma bint 'Amr of the Najjar clan of the Khazraj tribe of the city of Yathrib, later known as Medina. Abd al-Muttalib was born and raised in Medina. His uncle, Muttalib brought him to Mecca after the death of his father Hasim, he acquired the name 'Abd al-Muttalib "the slave of Muttalib," because when he arrived sitting on the back of his uncle's camel he was mistaken for his servant.

Abd al-Muttalib had a dream one day sleeping in the Hiijr Ismail next to the Kaba where Hagar and Ismail are buried. Muttalib was led to rediscover the well of Zam Zam by digging under the spot where the Quraysh had traditionally conducted their sacrifices. The location of the well was unknown at that time.

Due to his rediscovering the well Muttalib was placed with the rights of supplying the pilgrims to Mecca with water. His son al-'Abbas inherited the rights. During the time of Muttalib rediscovering of the well of Zam Zam he fathered one son named Harith. Al-Muttalib prayed to G-d for ten sons and promised that he would sacrifice one of them. His prayers were answered and when the time came he was willing to sacrifice his son Abdu Allah, who became the father of Prophet Muhammad (*saw*). Muttalib did not sacrifice his son Abdu Allah, instead he sacrificed one hundred camels.

Antar ibn Shaddad (d. 615 AD) became known as the "Father of Heroes." Antar was born of a slave mother among the Bedouins who traced their ancestry from Ishmael, son of Abraham and Hagar. His father was a chief of the Abs tribe. At the age of fifteen Antar entered into a battle with a neighboring tribe and came out a hero. Antar became known as a great warrior and poet. One of his poems was accorded the highest honor possible to a Muslim writer. It is hung up at the entrance to the great Masjid at Mecca. There were only six other poems so honored. Prophet Muhammad *(saw)* declared that Antar was the only Bedouin he ever admired. In 1889 Antar's works were published in thirty-two volumes in Cairo. Antar was as skilled in the poetic art as well as with the use of the sword. Deprived of the advantages of good looks at birth, he won merit by force of his soul, by the power of his spirit, and the indomitable energy of his character, occupying the foremost rank among men.

People of African Heritage in Islamic History during the time of the Prophet

U mm Aiman was the African girl who took Muhammad to his grandfather Abdul Muttalib when Muhammad's mother passed away. Aiman later married Zaid ibn Harith after his divorce with Zaynab who was later married to Prophet Muhammad (*saw*).

Among the first three converts to Islam was Prophet Muhammad's *(saw)* wife Khadija, his cousin Ali of African heritage, and a freed slave of African heritage Zaid ibn Harith.

Bilal Al-Habashi ibn Rabah was the first *muezzin*, the caller to prayer of Al-Islam. Bilal was also the first minister of finance and treasurer-general of the Muslim State under the leadership of Prophet Muhammad (*saw*). Bilal was bushy haired, tall, and dark. When Bilal died he was buried in Damascus, Syria, where his tomb is still venerated today. The Khalifa Omar (*sa*) stated that Bilal alone was worth a third of all Islam.

Ali ibn Abu Talib (*sa*) (598-661 AD) was a member of the house of Hashim, a cousin of the Prophet, also his son-in-law, the fourth Caliph, and one of the first converts to Al-Islam. Ali became renowned as a warrior during the early days of Islam. Ali married the Prophet's daughter Fatimah and had two sons, Hasan and Husayan, a third son Muhsin died in infancy, and a daughter Zaynab. After Fatimah died Ali had another son Muhammad ibn Hanafiyyah by his concubine. Ali was challenged for the office as the Caliph by Mu'awiyah, and was forced to set up his authority at Kufah in Iraq. When Ali was assassinated by Ibn Mulhim, Ali's son Hasan succeeded his father as the Caliph for about six months, but was then forced to cede the Caliphate to Mu'waiyah.

Zaid ibn Harith and **Umm Aiman** had a son Usamah. Both Zaid and Usamah ibn Zaid ibn Harith proved to be great generals in the wars with the Byzantine Greeks. Zaid was a slave given to the Prophet by his wife Khadijah. Later the Prophet freed him and adopted him as a son. Zaid had most of the task of collecting the Qur'an into one volume. He was one of the scribes used by the Prophet to write much of the revelation down after the Prophet would receive them.

Usamah ibn Zaid was the son of Zaid and Aiman. Usamah led a military expedition against the tribe of Bani Murrah. Usamah was seventeen at the time of this expedition. He also fought in the battle of the Ditch with the Muslim army. Usamah was made the commander of the army when he was eighteen years old. He was appointed by the Prophet (*saw*) as an example for the youth of Islam to carry the burden of great responsibility. Nineteen days after the Prophet's death Usamah led out his expedition to the borders of the Byzantine's territory. The Muslims under the command of Usamah were victorious in all their encounters with the enemy.

Abu Maria Anjashah Al-Habashi was trusted with taking care of the family of the Prophet *(saw)* especially in times of travel. Abu Maria was an Abyssinian set free by the Prophet and became the Prophet's "*Maula*" contractual brother.

Rabaah was a freed black slave and contractual brother of the Holy Prophet. When somebody wanted audience of the Prophet it was Rabaah who would ask the Prophet for permission to bring them in his private room.

Afga was an African who was the first to die in the holy wars of the Prophet. **El-Migda** was the first to fight in the holy war as a horseman. **Julaibib** died in a battle after valiantly killing seven men, and he was buried by the Prophet's own hands. **Said ibn Jubair** was known as a very pious man who was highly esteemed for his profound knowledge of the traditions of Prophet Muhammad (*saw*).

Shuqraan Saalih was a very honest man and liked by the Holy Prophet (*saw*). Shuqraan was entrusted with important things. He embraced Islam very early at Mecca, and migrated to Madinah. In the battle of Banul-Mustaliq (5 AH / 629 AD) all the captives were entrusted to Shuqrann. When the Prophet passed away Shuqraan participated in the funeral washing of his body. He was also left with something handsome from the bequest of the Prophet. Shuqraan died during the caliphate of Umar.

Akym ibn Akym and **Montagi ibn Nabhan** were both Ethiopians who taught the Syrians sciences. Montagi came to Arabia as a child and left it with a complete knowledge of Arabic and a pierced ear.

The first Muslim migration was in 615 CE / 620 AD, when a few Muslims traveled to Abyssinia. The Abyssinia Negus As'hama gave them refuge. Years later after the conquest of Mecca, seventy Muslim Abyssinian converts came to visit Mecca and the Prophet (*saw*) with some of the early immigrants. The Prophet's daughter Ruqayyah and her husband Uthman were among those who immigrated to Abyssinia.

The first Islamic incursion into Africa was in 640 AD, when General Amru captured Egypt. In 642 AD Alexandria surrendered. The conquest of North Africa was completed in 708 AD, when Musa Ibn Nusair subdued Morocco.

A Moor from Spain and West Africa

People of African Heritage
in Islamic History

General **Tarik Ibn Ziyad** was a Berber who converted to Islam, and in 9 AH / 711 AD crossed the straits and landed in Spain. He landed near the "rock" at the southern end of the Iberian Peninsula. The "Rock" ever since then has been known as the "Jabal Tariq" (the mountain of Tariq), also known as the "Rock of Gibraltar." Tarik and his army of African Berbers surprised and captured several Spanish towns. After several battles, the Spanish leader Roderick developed an army more than twice the size of Tarik's. Tarik told his troops, "Men! Before you is the enemy and the sea is at your backs. By Allah there is no escape for you save in valor and resolution." Tarik became Spain's Master and the Rock of Gibraltar bears his name.

Tarik marched towards Toledo, the capital, taking Ecija on the way. Another column took Archidona, a third seized Elvira, and a foirth, led by Mughith al Rumi took Cordova. The following year they conquered Madinah, Sidonia, Carmona, Seville, and Merida. The conquest of Saragosa sealed the fate of Spain, which the Muslims renamed Al Andalus. The Muslims also continued their march into France until they reached Poitiers Tours in 732 AD. Two years later in 734 AD, they conquered Lyons, Narbonne, and most of the area of the Provence down to the Mediterranean. In 217/832, the Muslims seized the island of Sicily and ruled it until the arrival of the Normans in 458/1058 AD. Tarik was the first Muslim who formulated the Sufi Doctrine of Ecstacy or the merging of one's soul with G-d.

Ibrahim Al-Mahdi (790 AD) was one of Islam's greatest singers of love songs. Prophet Muhammad's *(saw)* grandfather was the brother of Ibrahim's great-great-grandfather. Ibrahim's brother on his father side, was the great **Harun Al Rashid**, whose name is immortalized in the splendor of the Arabian Night's. Ibrahim, for a short period of time, was made ruler of Syria.

Ibrahim was known for his great merit and was a perfect scholar. He was a generous man with an open heart. He was proclaimed Caliph at Bagdad under the title of Al-Mubarak, "Blessed."[8] Its' been reported that Ibrahim was a prince with great talent as a singer and an able hand with musical instruments. He was also an agreeable companion at parties. He had 7,000 eunuchs in his army, 4,000 of them being white.

Dhul-Nun Al-Misri (180-245 AH / 796-859 AD) was a black Egyptian Sufi who had great knowledge of alchemy and arcane sciences. Alchemy was a meta-physical science which preceded the modern day science of chemistry. He is reputed to have been a link in the transmission of the spiritual sciences of ancient Egyptian Hieroglyphics. Dhul-nun was a pivotal figure in the origin and formation of Sufi mystic doctrine of ecstacy or the merging of one's soul with G-d. His teaching was first recorded and systematized by Al-Junayd of Baghdad in 297 AH.

Al-Jahiz's (776-868 AD) full name was Abu Uthman amr bin Bahr al Fukaymi Al-Basri Al-Jahiz. Al-Jahiz was the grandson of Amr bin Bahr. Al Jahiz was a prolific writer of books. In his book *Kitab-al-Hawaya* there contains theories of evolution, adaptation, and animal psychology. Al-Jahiz knew how to obtain ammonia from animal offal by dry distillation. He published theories on zoology, anthropology, theology, philosophy and other sciences. He wrote over 200 pieces of works, 120 of them were books. Among some of his works included such masterpieces as the seven volumes of, *The Book of Animals*, *The Book of Eloquence and Rhetoric*, *The Superiority of Speech Over Silence*, *Kitab Al-Sudan Wa-Bidan: The Superiority in Glory of the Black Race over the White*, and others. Al-Jahiz wrote, that the sons of Abd al-Muttalib, the grandfather of Prophet Muhammad, were black.

Other great African poets during Al-Jahiz's time were, **Abu Dulama Zend,** a poet, clown, court jester, and the Rabelais of his age; **Khair an-Nassaj**, a noted acentric and Sufi doctor died in 934 AD; **Abu'l Hassan Ibn Ismael; Al-Kanimi; Ibn Kalakis; Al-Khadi ar Rashid;** and **Nusaib Ibn Riar.**

Kafur Al-Ikshidi (d 967AD) was known as Kafur the Magnificent, the ruler of Egypt. Kafur was a slave who became a ruler. He was a forerunner of a long dynasty of slave kings, the Mamluks "a bondsman," one owned by another, some of whom were black. Kafur was the regent of Abdul Amyr, the new sultan, who was a child at the time, which made Kafur the virtual ruler. Kafur was known for his military genius, who twice defeated the renowned Sauf Eddaulah, the Emir of Aleppo.

Once Kafur led a successful expedition into Greece. Under Kafur's guidance Egypt became stronger than at any time since Cleopatra. Abdul Amyr, the young sultan, did not live long, and Ikshidi's second son Ali, was named to succeed him with Kafur as regent. When Ali died, Kafur put the next heir aside and seized the throne in his own name. Kafur had been ruling with such wisdom and kindness that his ugliness was quite forgotten. Kafur ruled for twenty-two years. He was a patron of knowledge and of the arts. He built libraries, schools, parks, and for himself a magnificent palace. He attracted writers, poets, astronomers, mathematicians, and philosophers to his court. It was second in the east only to that of the Caliph of Bagdad.

'Abdu Allah ibn Yasin al-Gazuli (d 1059 AD) was founder of the Al-Moravid movement. Between 1053 AD and 1061 AD a large part of northwestern Africa was under Al-Moravid which started as an Islamic movement. Almoravid is the Spanish name for the Arabic word *al-Murabitun* which means "those who stand together for the defense of religion." The Almoravid dynasty rose up from Berber tribes of the Sanhaja (Sahara) and tribes from Niger, and the Mali region. The empire was created after the death of 'Abd Allah ibn Yasin. Under Abd Allah ibn Yasin, the Al-Murabitun movement conquered the Gadala, Lemtuna, and Messufa Berber clans in southern Morocco, and brought Islam to the ancient kingdom of Ghana.

Yusuf Ibn Tashfin (d 500 / 1108 AD) was the founder of the city of Marrakesh in Morocco in 454 AH / 1062 AD, and the leader of the Almoravids in their conquest of Morocco and Spain. In 1086 AD Yusuf invaded Spain and within four years they conquered the area between the Tagus (Tajo) and Ebro rivers and set up viceroys in Seville and Granada. Upon returning from Spain, Yusuf ibn Tashfin, the Berber leader, was declared the emir by the councils of both the eastern and western region of the Almoravid dynasty. The dynasty was first divided between two leaders Abu Bakr ibn Omar, who held control over the movement from 448 AH / 1056 AD, and his cousin Yusuf ibn Tashfin, who seized Morocco in 453 AH /1061AD Yusuf's empire stretched from Senegal in the south to the Atlantic on the west, to Algeria and Tunis in the northeast, and Spain. In 483 AH./1090 AD., four years after he was invited to fight in Spain, Yusuf returned to Muslim Spain and captured the country for himself.

Yusuf was known as the Sultan of Africa. He died in 1108 AD at the age of 101. Yusuf was said to have dark circles around his eyes, woolly hair, and was tall, dark, handsome, and brave. The Almoravids ruled from 448-541 AH / 1056-1147 AD. The Almoravids originated from around Timbuctoo. Their empire stretched from Senegal in the south to the Atlantic on the west, and included Algeria and Tunis, an area larger than western Europe.

Abd-al-Mumin was a Berber and the founder of the *al-Muwahhid* (Almohads) dynasty. *Al-Muwahhid* is the arabic word for (Almohads) which in Arabic means **"one who proclaims the unity of G-d."** Almohad was the Spanish name of the Moorish dynasty and religious movement which ruled Morocco and Spain from (667-1269 AD). Al-Mumin succeeded the founder of the Al-Muwahhid, Muhammad ibn Tumart.

Abd-al-Mumin conquered Morocco 1140-1147 AD and other parts of North Africa. He put an end to the rule of the Almoravids. By 1154 AD he ruled Islamic Spain and part of Portugal. The Almohad period saw the heights and the end of Muslim philosophy in the west in the person of Ibn Tufay (d. 588 AH / 1185 AD) and Ibn Rushd (d.595 AH / 1198 AD).

It was also the period of **Ibn 'Arabi** (d. 638 AH / 1240 AD), the great metaphysician from Murcia in southern Spain. In craftsmanship and architecture the Almohads introduced a powerful style which marked a new beginning for Moorish art and was seen particularly in the Almohad arch. The monumental legacies of the Almohads are the Giralda, the vast cathedral of Seville, the Kutubiyyah mosque of Marrakesh, the Hasan mosque of Rabat, and what remains of the Almohad mosque at Tlemeen.

Yakub ibn Yusuf Al-Mansur (1149-1199 AD) was the greatest of the Moorish rulers of Spain. He ruled Spain in 1184 AD until his death in 1199 AD He was one of the notable leaders of the Almohads (Al-Muwahhid). Yakub aided the Sultan Saladin against the Crusaders. He defeated all his enemies and never lost a battle. Yakub's father and mother were of African heritage. Yakub came to the throne when his father Yakub ibn Abd el-Mumin was killed while besieging Santarem, Portugal in 1184 AD Yakub was responsible for the construction of numerous architectural monuments such as the Hassan Tower (minrat) in Rabat, Morocco. He built the city of Rabat, Alcassar, near Sallee, Mansura, and other cities. Mansur also built the famous Kasbah of Morocco as well as the Giralda in Seville, Spain. Mansur's kingdom stretched from the Atlantic along the Mediterranean to the borders of Egypt and included Mauritania, Morocco, Algeria, Tunis, Tripoli, the Balearic Islands, and most of Spain and Portugal.

Sundiata Keita (1210 -1260? AD) was the founder and ruler of the Mali Empire. Sundiata was the son of Nare Maghan, the ruler of Kangaba, a small state located on a tributary of the upper Niger river. In 1235 AD he led a coalition of Malinke' chiefs to victory in the Battle of Kirina. This victory was the beginning of the Mali Empire. Sundiata ruled Mali for twenty-five years, and expanded the state by incorporating the Ghana Empire and the West African gold fields. He built his capital at Niani.

Mansa Gonga-Musa (d. 1337) ruled Mali from 1312-1337 AD Musa was the grandson or grandnephew of the warrior king Sundiata, who first established Mali as a major empire in the thirteenth century. Musa extended it still further and ruled it at the height of its extent and power. Mansa (King) Musa is most famous for his 1324 AD Hajj pilgrimage to Mecca. Mali extended from the Atlantic Ocean to Gao on the middle Niger. After Mansa Musa came back from Hajj he hired Ibrahim-as-Saheli, an architect to improve upon the mosques, especially at Timbuktu, Jenne, and Kangaba. The buildings replaced the straw hut mosques with brick edifices, crenulated flat roofs, and pyramidal structures which varied from place to place. In 1325 AD the Manding under Gonga-Musa conquered Songhai.

Mansa Musa was succeeded by **Suleman** from 1336-1359 AD In Ibn Battutah's travels to Mali he stated that the Manding people and the administration of the state were efficient. He noted its prosperity, the courtesy and discipline of its officials and provincial governors, the excellent condition of public finances, the luxury, and rigorous complicated ceremonies of the royal receptions, the respect accorded to the decisions of justice, and to the authority of the sovereign. The finances were well organized. Taxation was imposed upon the royal domains, on minerals, on foreign trade, especially upon imports. In the judiciary there were representative lawyers, judges, and jurists. They exported gold, ivory, skins, and kola nuts, exchanged cattle, durra, and cotton.

Ibn Battutah (1304-1368 AD) was born in Tangiers, Morocco. He was an explorer and traveler known as the "Arab Marco Polo." Ibn Battutah's full name was Abu 'Abd Allah Muhammad ibn 'Abd Allah al-Lawati at-Tanji ibn Battutah. He was an ethnic Berber, and his family traced its ancestry to the nomadic Luwata tribe originating in Cyrenaica, west of the Nile Delta.

Ibn Battutah wrote poetry in addition to traveling across Africa, Arabia, Asia Minor, India, and China. He also traveled in Syria, Mesopotamia, Persia, East Africa, Oman, the Crimea, the regions of the Volga, Samarkand, Bukhara, Afghanistan, India, (in Delhi he became a Judge), Ceylon, Java, Sumatra, the Maldive Islands, Spain, and went across the Sahara to Timbuktu, and regions of the Niger.

For three years from 1352-1354 AD, Ibn Battutah traveled by camel on ancient caravan routes from oasis to oasis, and through major market towns. He stayed for months at a time with rulers in the kingdoms of Mali and Songhai, as well as with Tuareg pastoralists living in the Niger River basin. Ibn Battutah is the only traveler known to have visited all the Muslim-ruled lands of medieval times. His observations are renowned for their detail, credibility, and color.

Ibn Khaldun (1332-1406 AD) was born in Tunis, Tunisia. Ibn Khaldun wrote a monumental history about north Africa. He also made a significant contribution in his work on the Muqaddimah (Prolegomena), perhaps the first systematic philosophical study of history and society. The Muqaddimah not only recounted the history of the region's Berbers and Arabs, but also outlined a method for the historical study of society. While in Cairo, Ibn Khaldun taught at the famous Islamic University al-Azhar. He became a grand Maliki judge, and once again became embroiled in dynastic politics.

Ibn Khaldun was often called the "Father of Historiography" and the "Father of Sociology." His life was extremely turbulent. At one time he served the Merinid Sultan in Fez as a functionary. He had a post with the Sultan of Bujiya, and he was the Grand Qadi (Chief Judge) of the Maliki rite in Egypt. In each place he ran into problems. In some of the places he was imprisoned and in others he was thrown out the country.

Abu Hassan Ali (d 1357 AD) was known as the "El Sultan Aswad" or "The Black Sultan." He was the most famous of the Merinides rulers of Morocco. He was renowned in the annals of the east for his ambition, courage, and the fortitude with which he bore his suffering and distress, as well as for his patronage of art. Under his leadership the Moroccan art, architecture, and literature rose to the zenith of their splendor.

In 1330 AD Ali captured Gibraltar, and by the mid 1340s the kings of Castile and Portugal defeated him. They took not only his treasures but also his wives. Driven from Europe, he returned to Africa, conquered Tunis and Algeria, and became so great a power in north Africa that the Mameluke sultans of Egypt looked to him as the protector of the western gate of Islam.

Abu Abd-Allah known in the west as King Boabdil. Abd-Allah was the last Nasrid ruler of Granada. In 1492 AD Abu Abd-Allah was forced to give up the keys to the city and to leave with the Moors going into the mountains over to Africa. Some of his words on his way out after momentarily pausing was *"Allah-u-Akbar"* as he burst into tears.

Sunni Ali Ber (d 1492 AD) was the founder of the Empire of Timbuktu. In 1464 AD Sunni Ali became the leader of the Songhai Empire. Sunni Ali's real name was Ali Kolon. Ali began as a common soldier in the army of Kankan Musa, the Mandingo ruler of the Mellestine. In 1433 AD the Tuareg Chief Ali drove the Manding administration from Timbuktu. In 1468 AD the Songhay took the city of Timbuktu from the Tuareg, and then conquered Jenne and Massina in 1473 AD Sunni Ali was known as the "The Celebrated Infidel," "The Horrible Tyrant," and "The Great Oppressor."

Songhai had several flourishing cities, the principal being Jennie, which was strongly fortified and was one of the great commercial centers of Islam. Sunni Ali introduced the first use of a navy in an African military. Boats had been used before in African wars, but never before had a nation in these parts thought and planned the use of a navy for the conquest of the Niger and its defense. Sunni Ali was one of the most effective conquerors and organizers of Africa prior to the European conquest. Sunni defeated the Manding army and made the Songhai independent.

In 1492 A.D., on the way back from a battle while crossing a swelling current, Sunni Ali drowned. Sunni Ali was succeeded by his son, Abu Kebr, but one far worthier than he felt entitled to the throne. It was Mohammed ibn Abu Bakr, the favorite general of Sunni Ali. A year later Mohammed defeated Abu Kebr at Anghoke in one of the bloodiest battles in history.

Al-Hassan ibn Muhammad al-Wazzani al-Fasi (Leo Africanus) (1485-1554 AD). Al-Fasi was born in Spain and moved to Fes, Morocco as a child. He was from a Spanish speaking Moor of Granada during the reign of King Ferdinand and Queen Isabella of Spain. He was educated and worked for his uncle as a clerk. As a young man he traveled into the interior of African Sudan. His first trip was to the Songhai Empire in western Sudan, around 1512 AD During this trip he traveled throughout the region and visited the major trading cities like Timbuktu, Djenne, Gao, and Sijilmasa. He recorded his observation on the region's major states such as the Hausa, Bornu, and the Bulala, also the great empires of Songhai and Mali. Between 1516 -1518 AD Africanus made several trips to Egypt. In 1518 AD, on his return home from Egypt, he was captured and enslaved by some Christians off an island of Tunisia, sold and given to the Pope Leo X.

It was the Pope who gave him the name Leo Africanus. He wrote a book and completed it in 1526 AD, on the *History and Description of Africa and the Notable Things Therein Contained.*" It was finally published in 1550 AD and for two centuries the book provided much needed information for Europe on the history, geography, and the people of Africa. He was eventually freed by the Pope and baptized. He remained in Italy for at least 20 years before he returned back to North Africa. Africanus died in Tunis between 1552 and 1560 AD.

"Askia the Great," Mohammed Ture (d 1538 AD). In 1493 AD Mohammed ibn Abu Bakr seized the throne of Songhai, calling himself "The Prince of Believers"and the "Caliph of the Muslims." He became known as "Askia the Great." Mohammed made Songhai (Songhay) a great empire. He was a governor under Sunni Ali. Askia rebelled against Sunni Ali's son Abu Kebr. His reign was from 1493-1529 AD. He was the builder of the Empire of Timbuktu. In Songhai, Askia developed intellectual centers in Gao, Walata, Timbuktu, and Dijenne. To increase commerce he standardize measures and weights, created a regular army with a reserve unit, which left the rest of the population free to trade and carry on agriculture during the time of war.

Some of Askia's men came from as far north as the Barbary states. Along the mighty Niger River and its tributaries Askia built a navy, constructed harbors, and dug canals. To Askia's ports came ships from Portugal and the Mediterranean bringing goods in exchange for Songhai gold, copper, woods, and hides. Songhai caravans went to Cairo, Algiers, Morocco, and Bagdad. Under the leadership of Askia, the Songhai Empire flourished until it became one of the richest of that period. By 1538 AD, the empire stretched from the Atlantic to Lake Chad.

Timbuktu

Timbuktu became a real center of the Islamic world, and was known as the "Mecca of the Sudan" and "The Queen of the Sudan." In 1497 AD Askia went on Hajj pilgrimage to Mecca, and during that visit he received the title Khalifa for the Tekrur Sudan by the grand Sharif of Mecca.

Askia brought under his sway the kingdom of the Yollofs and the Mossis, as well as those of many minor kings and chiefs, until his realm extended beyond Lake Chad, and took six months to traverse from west to east.

In 1494 AD Omar, the brother of Askia Mohammed, conquered all of Massina, which included at the time the Fulani kingdom of the Diallo. Askia captured Bagana in 1498 AD, and conquered part of the kingdom of Diara in 1500 AD, and in 1506 AD he extended his sway as far as Galam, the Bakel on the Senegal. By 1529 AD Askia became blind and was dethroned by his son Mussa. Askia's grandson, David, the son of Mussa, was the leader of Songhai from 1549 AD to 1583 AD.

Ahmad Baba (1556-1627 AD) was born in Arawan, near Timbuktu. He was one of the best known Islamic scholars, jurist, and writers of his time. Ahmad was born into a prestigious Aqit family and was educated in Islamic theology and law. Over the course of his life he wrote more than fifty-six works on theology, Islamic jurisprudence, history, and Arabic grammar. More than half of these are still in existence, and several are used by West African scholars (*Ulama*). Ahmad was a great collector of books. He amassed a library containing thousands of books. During Ahmad's time Timbuktu was ruled by the Songhai Empire, which was renowned throughout the Islamic world as a center of learning.

In 1591 AD the Moroccans invaded Timbuktu. Ahmad and other scholars refused to serve the Moroccan rulers. In 1593 AD Ahmad and the other leading scholars were accused of starting a rebellion. They were arrested and deported to Marrakech in 1594 AD Reports state that the Moroccans confiscated several of the scholars' private libraries. Ahmad lost nearly 1,600 volumes. One of Ahmad's most famous works was *Kifayat al-Muktaj,* a biographical dictionary of Maliki legal scholar's jurists. After the death of the Sultan of Morocco, Ahmad was set free and returned back to Timbuktu. Ahmad wrote a catalogue of Islamic people and the peoples of the Sudan, which was used by Usman Dan Fodio.

Idris Alooma III ruled from 1570-1619 AD the African kingdom of Kanem-Bornu, located in central Sahara. Some of the earlier rulers of Kanem-Bornu were Ibrahim (1352-1376 AD), **Omar** (1394-1398 AD), and **Ali** (1472-1504 A.D.). Ali established the empire of Gassaro. His son **Idris II** recovered the Kanem. **Idris III** extended authority over Kano, Zinder, Kanem, Fitri, and to the south of Chad.

Mulai (Ismael) Ishmael (1647-1727 AD) was the son of a full-blooded black slave woman, and his father was Mulai Sharif, King of Tafilalet. His father had been captured by Omar, King of Sillec and thrown into prison. From this union came two children Rashid and Mulai Ismael, both of whom, in turn, became sultans of Morocco. Mulai defeated the Turkish commander and army at Fez, and conquered the Berbers of the Atlas. He pushed the white Christian powers entirely out of northwest Africa. He defeated the English at Tangiers and Fort Charles, and broke the hold of Spain on Africa.

Mulai crushed the Spaniards at Larache and drove them across the straits. Moroccan ships plundered the vessels and the coasts of Spain, France, and England, bringing back tens of thousands of white captives, who were held for ransom.

Among Mulai Ishmael's slaves was Alexander Selkrik, hero of Robinson Crusoe. Ishmael had a picked corp of 10,000 white warriors, captured or born into captivity, which he commanded himself. Mulai's favorite wife was Zidana, a full-blooded black woman. His second wife was an English woman who had been captured at the age of fifteen. His third wife was another black woman, Lela Coneta, who later raised her son Mohammed to be on the throne.

Mulai Ishmael was also known for his callousness and cruel disciplinarian. The finest monument to his memory is the Bab Mansour, which bears the inscription "The Asylum of the Weak and the Providence of the Needy; the King who is obeyed from Love and Respect."

Abram Hannibal (1670-1762 AD) was born in Eritrea. He was a slave of the Tsar Peter the Great. Hannibal eventually became a major general and military engineer in Russia. He entered Russia in 1700 AD and began his service with the royal court in 1705 AD He fought with the French army in 1718 AD and was captured by the Spanish and eventually released in 1722 AD. After 1725 AD he was placed in exile to Siberia for three years where he built a fortress. In the 1730s he married a German officer's daughter named Christina Von Shoberg, together they had 11 children. Their granddaughter Nadezhda gave birth to Alexander Pushkin, the father of modern Russian literature.

Abu-l-Abbas Ahmad Tijani (1737-1815 AD) was a north African who founded the Sufi "Tijanya" order. Ahmad studied the religious sciences in Tlemeen, Cairo, Mecca, and Fez. He joined several other *turuq* (religious brotherhoods) before founding his own religious brotherhood (tariqah). The tomb of Ahmad is in the heart of Fez, Morocco near the Qarawiyyin Masjid. There are two special du'a prayers that are used by the Tijanis, "The Prayer of Victory," and the "Jewels of Perfection."

Uthman (Usman) dan-Fodio (1754-1817 AD) was the founder of the Sokoto Caliphate, the Tukulor empire, and was one of the best known Qadiriya and Fulani scholars. He was born in the Hausa state of Gobir. Uthman studied the Qur'an with his father, an eminent scholar and Sufi. At the age of 25 he begin teaching and preaching Islam. In 1786 AD Uthman led a successful Islamic moral reform movement. Uthman criticized the Hausa ruling elite for their heavy taxation and other practices that he claimed violated Islamic laws. Uthman was a Muslim who gained wide spread reputation as a very educated and spiritually minded Imam.

In 1801 AD Uthman became aware of the problems between the Fulani shepherds of Gober and their Hausa patrons. Afterward in 1804 AD he declared holy war against the inhabitants and their neighbor, taking the part of the Fulani, who spoke the same language as that of his people. He enlisted a large number of soldiers among the Futa Toro, the Massina, the Liptako, and the Songhai and set out with an army with which he conquered most of Hausa. Uthman made Sokoto his capital. In 1808 AD Gobir, the capital, and Alkalawa fell to Uthman. He soon expanded his empire to include all of the Hausa kingdoms, a part of the Adamwa, the Nupe, the Kebbi, and the Liptako in the bend of the Niger.

In 1812 AD Uthman withdrew into private life, writing many works on the proper conduct of the pious Islamic community. In 1812 AD Uthman divided up the Caliphate with his brother Abdullahi, who took over the control of the western provinces and other possessions, and to his son Muhammad the eastern emirates. Muhammad Bello succeeded him and became the ruler of the Tukulor empire and the Sokoto Caliphate, then the largest independent state in Africa south of the Sudan during the 19th century.

Muhammad Bello (1781-1837 AD) ruled the Tukulor empire from 1815-1839AD Muhammad was the son of Uthman dan-Fodio. He made a great impression upon his time with his poems and prose works in Arabic, dealing with historical and religious problems of his day. He was born in Gobir in present day Nigeria in 1781 AD and died in 1837 AD in Sokoto in present-day Nigeria. In 1817 AD after the death of his father Muhammad assumed the overall leadership of the Sokoto Caliphate as the "Commander of the Faithful."

During his reign Bello consolidated the empire and soothed internal conflicts between the Hausa and the Fulani leadership by constructing an impartial justice system. He commissioned a network of fortresses for the caliphate's defense along the border with the Kanem-Bornu empire. Under Bello, Sokoto's forces raided and enslaved people in the south. These slaves provided the agricultural labor that generated much of the caliphate's revenue. Bello was succeeded by his brother Abu Bakr Atiku.

Al-Hajj Umar ibn Siid Tal (1794-1864 AD) was born in Halwar (Fouta Tora) in present day Senegal and died near Hamdalahi in present day Mali. He was a Muslim Imam and founder of the Tukulor Empire of present day Mali. Beginning in 1804 AD Umar led jihads against the emirs of Hausaland, eventually forging the Sokoto Caliphate, the largest state in the 19th century.

Hajj Umar Tal's religious movement popularized the Tijaniya Sufi order and influenced reformers throughout the 19th century in West Africa. Umar was influenced by the teachings of the Tijaniya brotherhood at an early age. In 1837 AD Umar moved to the Fouta Dijallon region. Umar acquired firearms by selling non-Muslim captives to the French.

In 1852 AD Umar mobilized his followers and launched the first of several jihads in the Senegal and Niger River valleys. In Umar's early campaigns into the area he easily conquered some of the smaller city states and kingdoms, which he united under the rule of his sons.

In the late 1850s, he met opposition from the French, who feared his growing empire as a threat to their trade and future colonization. After many battles with the French, by the early 1860s Umar was defeated by the Bambara kingdom of Se'gu, once an allied of Umar's kingdom.

In 1864 AD Umar died in a fire that was set by his enemies, leaving the empire to his sons.

Umar's son, Mustafa ruled from 1864-1870 AD, followed by his brother Ahmadu. Under both sons the empire was losing ground. In 1891 AD the empire fell to the French and Ahmadu was forced to flee.

Abd al-Qadir (1807-1883 AD) was an Algerian religious and military leader credited with unifying Algerian territory into a state. Abd al-Qadir is considered a hero of anti-colonial resistance. He created an Arab-Berber alliance to oppose the French expansion from 1830s-1840s. In 1826 AD Abd al-Qadir and his father made Hajj. In 1837 AD France signed a treaty with al-Qadir called the "Treaty of Tafna." It acknowledged his sovereign authority over an area encompassing two thirds of Algeria. By 1843 AD the French abandoned the treaty.

Hamid ibn Mohammed "Tippu Tib" (1837-1905 AD) was one of the most powerful traders in central and east Africa in the late 19th century. Starting from his birthplace, the island of Zanzibar, Tippu crossed Africa by way of Lake Tanganyika, up through the vast stretch of what is now the Republic of the Congo. Tippu Tib was a trailblazer for the great explorers of Africa. In the path that he blazed, Stanley and Livingstone followed.

"Tippu Tib"

Tippu's career began when he was twelve years old, when he would go with his father on trading trips. At the age of twenty-three in 1850, he set out on his own. Tib traded slaves and ivory for firearms and his large caravans also served as his personal armies and hunting bands.

Tippu accumulated incredible wealth and power, expanding his territorial control through raids as well as deals with regional chiefs and other traders. By the early 1880s he was the most powerful trader in central and east Africa. His caravans traveled from Zanzibar on the east coast to Kasongo on the west coast of the Lualaba River. They raided villages for slaves in the central African forest. Many of his captives were put to work cultivating sugar cane, rice, and maize on plantations near the town of Kasongo and Nyangwe. In 1885 AD Leopold II of Belgium claimed control over the Congo free State, which included Tippu Tib's empire. He was able to negotiate governorship of what is now the eastern Democratic Republic of the Congo.

Samori (Samory) Toure' (1830?-1900 AD) was born at Bissandugu in the Beyla region of Guinea. His father was Lafia Ture and his mother was Massokono Kamara, both were Mandingoes. He was known as the Napoleon of the Sudan. Samori was an empire builder and fighter against French colonialism.

By 1870 AD Samori forged a large private army, and eventually conquered an area reaching from the Fouta Dijallon in the west to the Asante country of Ghana in the east. Samori established his capital at Bissandougou in what is now Cote D'Ivoire. At the age of twenty Samori came home one day to find out that warriors from Konia had raided his community and carried off his mother as a captive to their chief, Sori-Ibrahima. Samori went to the chief to plead for her release but suffered enslavement himself.

While in the service of Sori-Ibrahima, Samori distinguished himself as a soldier and hero in the military. Samori was given the chance to become the commander in chief of the army, yet he chose the freedom of his mother and himself. Toure went back home and worked for a short time before he became a military leader. Samori gave his service to Bitiki Suane, the king of Torongo, who he supplanted and became king. He defeated Sori-Ibrahim and became ruler of Konia. He then went forward in conquest for eight years and established an empire of 400,000 square kilometers. In his conquest included the land of the Kanadugu, the Bisandugu, the Konia, and parts of the Wasulu.

Samori had Masajid (Mosques) built in each city and made Islam the state religion. The army had ten divisions and the generals were governors of the corresponding ten provinces. In 1898 AD Samori was taken prisoner and deported to Gabon with his son Sarankieni Mori, and two years later died at the age of sixty-five.

Mohammed Ahmed ibn Abdullah "The Mahdi" (1844-1885 AD) was a native of Khanag, Dongola, Sudan. By the 1860s the Mahdi, at the age of twelve, was known for reciting whole parts of the Qur'an. Mohammed's parents' names were like Prophet Muhammad's *(saw)* parents Abdullah and Aminah. His teacher was Mohammed Sherif. One day he became a local hero among the community poor when he challenged the rich to stop their waste and to help the poor.

As a young man many people were impressed with Mohammed's politeness and his willingness to help the women with their heavy water buckets. Soon people started saying he was the expected Messiah. In 1870 AD he began to teach on his own at Aba Island on the White Nile.

In 1881 AD Muhammad had a series of visions that convinced him that he was the Mahdi. He proclaimed himself the Mahdi and in the same year made hijra from Aba Island to the Nuba Mountains. After a couple of early victories against the Egyptians, from the hills and plains, deserts and forests, the tribes rallied to the black flag of the Mahdi. Tens of thousands of people joined him from tribes like the Selem, Baggara, Risega, Homer, Dinka, Bongo, Madi, and Bari.

Mahdi became the controlling force in his day of eastern Sudan. He began his career with the defeat of Rashid-Bey, the governor of Fashoda, in the southern Kordofan in 1882 AD In 1883 AD he gained control of the capital El-Obeid, and the governors of Darfur, Bahr-el-Ghazal, and Lupton-Bey surrendered to him.

In 1885 AD the Mahdi seized Omdurman, a suburb of Khartum, then days later Khartum itself was seized. During his short period of governance, the Mahdi used the Qur'an and the traditions concerning Prophet Muhammad *(saw)* as his primary legal guide. His followers held him in such esteem that they fought for the water in which he bathed and scraped up the earth over which he walked, keeping it as sacred. He kept his word to his people. He had expensive brocades and costly silks cut up as garments for the people. It was Mohammed who freed the people from sixty years of slavery and cruel taxation by the British and he Egyptians. He defeated every combined British and Egyptian army sent against him. In

1885 AD, six months after conquering Omdurman, the Mahdi became stricken with typhoid fever and died on June 22, 1885.

Ahmed Ben Musa (Bu-Ahmed) (d.1900 AD) was the last great ruler of Morocco, also known as the Iron Chancellor. He was a slave born in the palace of the sultan. He grew up with the heir to the throne Mulai Hassan. Ahmed was made court chamberlain, confidant, and finally sultan under Mulai Hassan. Bu-Ahmed came into absolute power in 1894 AD, when the young sultan did as he was advised.

As a keen lover of art and learning, Bu Ahmed fostered learning and sent promising students away to learn. Bu-Ahmed provided one of the most stable governments in Morocco that it had seen in years. He also built a palace as Morocco had never seen. For twenty years Musa kept the wolves of the western world and the Europeans at bay. He died in 1900 AD., and his death marked an end to the last of the great Muslim empires in Africa. They described Bu Ahmed as a little fat man with short legs, an enormous stomach that gave it a rolling movement, dark skinned, who was once a slave.

Amadou Bamba Mbacke (1850-1927AD) was the founder of the order of the sufi brotherhood of the (Mouride) Muridiyya of Senegal around 1905, an offshoot of the Qadiriyya order. He was a Wolof teacher, who came from a scholarly family at the court of the king of Kayor. He was a nonpolitical sufi leader. The French exiled him, first to Gabon in 1895 AD, then in 1902 AD to Mauritania, where he rejoined Shaykh Sidiya. In 1912 AD Bamba was allowed to return home where he settled in Diourbel, in Baol. After his death he was succeeded by his son Mustafa Mbacke'.

The Muridiyya ethos of labor and organization of their students into communities of workers of agricultural and other labor services helped make the Muridiyya order an important economic factor in Senegal.

Amath Ba (Maba Diakhou) was the son of N'Dougou Penda Ba, a Qur'anic scholar who spent his life teaching Islam at Badiku to the Wolof people. Ma Ba began a revolt in 1861 at the village Badish.

Some Muslims of the African Diaspora in the Americas and the Caribbean

In The United States

Many slaves knew how to read and write Arabic before their capture. The earliest known writer was Job in 1734. He wrote the Qur'an down three times from memory, and other items. In 1753 two Moors (Muslims) from Morocco in South Carolina wrote the local government for their freedom in Arabic. In 1768 another Muslim living in South Carolina wrote four Surahs from the Qur'an. He was the slave of Captain David Anderson. There are at least nine different people reported to have written Arabic text during this period. Below, among the twelve Muslims we talk about at least five of them left some Arabic writings behind and at least two were war heroes.

In 1730 AD **Job ibn Solomon ibn Dijallo (Jallo)** came from Bundu, Senegal. He was captured in 1730 in Gambia and brought to Annapolis, MD in 1731, where he was purchased. He was a Fulani who lived near the banks of the Gambia river in Senegal. The Gambia river was the only river the European traders could sail for any distance, which lead them further south along the coast.

Job was enslaved in Annapolis, Maryland for about four years. Afterward he was sent to London where he was finally set free and sent back home to work for the Royal African Company of London in his homeland. Job came from a family of Alpha "Imams." While in London he wrote down three copies of the Qur'an from memory. As a slave Job was allowed a place to pray and other conveniences in order to make his slavery as easy as possible. Reports about Job describe him as a well-mannered, courtly, intelligent, monotheistic, and a literate human being.

In 1730 **Lamine Jay** came from Futa-Toro, Senegal. He was captured along with Job ibn Soliman ibn Dijallo (Jallo) trading on the lower part of the Gambia river. Lamine was also brought to Annapolis, Maryland where he became known as a Linguist. In less than five years Jay was able to win his freedom and return home with the help of his friend Job.

In 1767 **Kunta Kinte** was captured and enslaved. Kunta Kinte was born in 1750, in the village of Juffure in Gambia. He was shipped to Annapolis, Maryland on the ship Lord Ligonier and sold to a Virginia planter. Kunta Kinte fought hard to hold on to his Islamic heritage. Alex's Haley book *Roots* talks about Kunta Kinte and his life.

In 1790 **Yusef Ben Ali** was known as Joseph Benenhaly from North Africa. His name appears in the 1790 census of Sumter county, South Carolina. General Thomas Sumter recruited Joseph Benenhaly, of Arab descent, and another man known as John Scott to fight with him in the American Revolution. Originally, it is believed that they were pirates. After the war, Sumter took them inland with him to near Stateburg where they settled down and many of their descendants have remained. His dark-skinned descendants became known as the Turks of Sumter County because of their Moorish background.

In 1803 **Bilali (Ben Ali) Muhammad** and his family arrived in Georgia on Sapelo Island. Bilali Muhammad was a Fula from Timbo Futa-Jallon in present day Guinea-Conakry. By 1806 he became the plantation manager for Thomas Spalding, a prominent Georgian master. Bilali and his wife Phoebe had twelve sons and seven daughters. His daughters' names were Margaret, Hester, Charlotte, Fatima, Yoruba, Medina, and Bint. All his daughters except Bint could speak English, French, Fula, Gullah, and Arabic. Bilal was well educated in Islamic law. While enslaved Bilali became the community leader and Imam of at least eighty men. Bilali "Ben Ali" was the leader of one of America's earliest known Muslim communities. During the War of 1812 Bilali told his slave master that he had eighty men of the true faith to help defend the land against the British. Ben Ali was the leader from 1806 to the late 1830s.

Bilali was known for regularly wearing his fez, a long coat, praying five times a day facing the east, fasting during the month of Ramadan, and celebrating the two holidays when they came. Bilali was buried with his Qur'an and prayer rug. In 1829 Bilali wrote a thirteen page hand written book called a *Risala* (letter) about some of the laws of Islam and Islamic living. The book is known as *Ben Ali's Diary*, housed today at the University of Georgia in Athens.

In 1803 **Salih Bilali (Old Tom)** came from a powerful family of Massina in the Temourah district in west Africa. He was captured around 1782, sold in the Bahamas at first and then in the US around 1803. He lived from 1770-1846. He was sold to John Couper in the Bahamas and brought to St. Simon Island, GA. From 1816-1840 Salih Bilali was the trusted head slave manager of more than 450 slaves of John and Hamilton Couper. It was reported by his master's son, that while Salih was on his death bed, his last words were "Allah is G-d and Mohammed his Prophet (*saw*)."

One of Salih's descendants was Robert Abbott, founder of the "Chicago Defender," one of the nation's first black newspapers. Another one of Salih's descendants was named after him, Bilali Sullivan who was known as (Ben Sullivan). Bilali (Ben) Sullivan purchased some of the original property of the plantation in 1914. He was interviewed about his life in the 1930s.

In 1807 **Yarrow (Mamout) Marmood** was given his freedom. Yarrow was enslaved and brought from Guinea, West Africa before the American Revolution. Yarrow was given his freedom by Upton Beall of Montgomery County in the Washington, DC area. Upton Beall's deed was recorded on April 13, 1807, which stated that the Negro Yarrow was given his freedom because he was more than forty-five years old and that he would not become a bother to the County of Washington.

In the 1800-1810 census Yarrow's name was listed as Negro Yarrow with a wife or elderly woman living with him. In the 1820 census Yarrow's name was listed as Yarrow Marmood with a woman living with him. Yarrow Marmood was a property owner in the Georgetown area in Washington, DC. Yarrow established a hauling business, owned real estate on what is now 3330-3332

Dent Place NW, and invested some of his savings in the stock of the Bank of Columbia. One of Yarrow's neighbors and friend was another manumitted slave named Joseph Moor who became a respectable grocer in Georgetown.

On April 12, 1844, Yarrow's estate was administered by probate court in Washington, DC, under the name Negro Yarrow. Yarrow lived to be more than 100 years old. The dates of his birth and death have been record as 1736-1844.

In 1807 **Hajj Omar Ibn Sayyid** was captured at the age of thirty-seven. Omar was a Fula born in Fur Tur in present day Senegal. He was born from a Serahule family. Omar lived from 1770-1864. He studied in Bundu, Senegal where he learned how to read and write arabic, Islamic studies, and made Hajj in Mecca before his capture. Omar was enslaved in Charleston, SC where he labored for a short period of time before he escaped in 1810 to Fayetteville, NC where he was caught and imprisoned. While in prison Omar persuaded James Owen, a general in the state militia and brother of John Owen (who later became Governor of North Carolina), to purchase him, which he did for $900.00. Omar was also known as Uncle Moreau.

Omar ibn Sayyid wrote many items in Arabic while enslaved. He wrote the Lords Prayer, the Bismillah, this is How You Pray, Quranic phases, the 23rd Psalm, and Omar's latest known writing was in 1857 Surah 110 of the Holy Qur'an. Omar was given an Arabic written Bible and a Qur'an by his slave master. The Bible is housed today at Davidson College in North Carolina.

In 1828 **Abraham Abdul Rahman ibn Sori** (1762–1829) was set free by the order of the Secretary of State Henry Clay and President John Quincy Adams. He was born in Timbo, West Africa (in present day Guinea). He was known as the "Prince of Slaves." He was a Fulbe from the land of Futa Jallon. Abraham left Futa in 1774 to study in Mali at Timbuktu.

Abraham was captured by warring tribes and sold to slave traders in 1788 at the age of twenty-six. He was bought by a Natchez, Mississippi cotton and tobacco farmer, where he eventually became the overseer of the plantation of Thomas Foster. In 1794 he married Isabella, another slave of Foster's, and eventually fathered a large family. In 1807 a coincidental meeting took place. John Cox, an Irish ship's surgeon, whose life had been saved by Abraham's father many years earlier recognized the Prince in the market, learned of his story, and began petitioning for his freedom.

In 1826 nearly twenty years later he wrote a letter to his relatives in Africa. A local newspaperman sent a copy to Senator Thomas Reed in Washington, who forwarded it to the U.S. Consulate in Morocco. After the Sultan of Morocco read the letter, he asked President Adams and Secretary of State Henry Clay to release Abraham Abdul Rahman.

In 1828 at the age of sixty-six Abraham gained his freedom. Rahman had been a slave in America for forty years before he got his freedom. Rahman and his wife sailed for Africa in February 1829. The following September his former owner died. Foster's heirs sold two of Rahman's children and five of his grandchildren to the American Colonization Society (A.C.S), and they were reunited with his wife in Liberia.

In 1835 **Lamen Kebe** known as (Old Paul) was liberated after having been in servitude in South Carolina and Alabama. Lamen Kebe was captured in battle and arrived in America in the early 1800s. He was from an elite class of Serahule who were trained to rule, advise, teach, protect, trade, translate, collect taxes, and travel. His family were the founders of ancient Ghana, and they were among the earliest converts to Islam south of the Sahara. His mother was a Mandinga. In Senegambia he was a schoolmaster in the land of the Fulah before his capture. Lamen and Omar Sayyid corresponded with each other in 1835 in Arabic. Lamen (Old Paul) through Omar, provided Theodore Dwight, a member of the American Ethnological Society, with information of his native land and school system. Lamen returned back to Africa at the age of sixty in 1835.

In 1860, **Muhammad Ali ibn Said** (1833-1882), known as "Nicholas Said," arrived in America as a free man. Muhammad was born in the Kingdom of Bornoo, West Africa near Lake Chad to a well-educated merchant family. Said was kidnaped and enslaved when he was sixteen. His first slave master was an Arab named

Abdel Kader who took him to Tripoli and Fezzan. Muhammad was then sold to Alexander Menshikov, an aide to the Russian Czar, then to Nicholas Trubetzkoy with whom he traveled to many places during his years of slavery from Russia, Rome, Persia to France. In 1860 he left Liverpool, England with a man from Holland to travel to Boston, New York, Kingston, New Providence, Toronto, Quebec, and other places in North America as a freed man.

In 1861 he arrived in Detroit. Shortly afterward he found a teaching job and in 1863 Muhammad enlisted in the 55th Massachusetts colored regiment and became a Civil War hero. He served faithfully and bravely with his regiment as Corporal and then Sergeant in the south. Near the close of the war he was assigned, at his own request, to the hospital department, to learn some knowledge of medicine. His Army records show that he died in Brownsville, Tennessee in 1882.

In 1864 **Captain Harry Dean** was born. He was the son of Susan Cuffe Dean whose brother was Paul Cuffe. Captain Dean's family came from Quata, Morocco. For three generations the family were wealthy merchants in Philadelphia. Captain Dean found the first black nautical training school in America. Dean maintained his family's Islamic tradition during his seafaring days on the ship "Pedro Gorino," and in southern Africa where he tried to build an African empire. He was also associated with the Muslim Mosque of London. In the United States he distributed Islamic literature in Chicago, Los Angeles, Seattle, and Washington state.

In Brazil

There is documentary evidence of the presence of the Mandinka Muslims in the early Americas. The Mandinka made contact with Brazil; they appeared to have used it as a base for exploration of the Americas. From Brazil, Muslim explorers went to the west and the north. They traveled along rivers in the dense jungles of South America. Inscriptions found in Brazil at Bahia and Minas Gerais, and on the coast of Peru at Yio, show a definite presence of the Mandinka Muslim Africans.

The inscriptions were originally written in the Vai and related Manding scripts. The early Muslim Mandinka penetrated Central and North America; they even inter-married with the Iroquois and Algonquian people.

In 1835 there was a Muslim uprising in Bahia, Brazil. The Muslims in Brazil formed the largest Islamic community in America. Most Muslims (Minas) adopted the outward signs of the religion that was imposed on them but secretly retained their own beliefs. In 1860 two Americans concurred, that the Muslims did not renounce their faith even after they had been baptized. Sylviana Diouf in her book, *Servants of Allah* states that the Muslim names found surviving in Brazil are Mohammad, Sule, Aluna, Sanim, Bilal, Musa, Ali, Usman, and Abdullah.

In the Caribbean

In the Caribbean when Columbus reportedly discovered the West Indies about 1493 CE, he found there a race of white people with wooly hair whom he called Caribs. They were seafaring hunters and tillers of the soil, peaceful and united. They hated aggression. Their religion was Mohammedanism (Islam) and their language presumably Arabic.

Ivan Van Seqtima in his book, *African Presence in Early America* points out that the proper names Califurnam and Garif are Mandinga variants of the Arabic *Khalifatu-'n-Nabi*, which in Mande becomes *Kalifa-nami* and can be shortened to Kalifa, or Karifa, or the Black Carib Garif. When the Spaniards arrived at St. Vincent they found there a "wooly-haired" people who were "Mohammedans," and whose language was presumably Arabic. The Carib dietary habits tend to support the Islamic tradition, it was only in recent time they added pork to their diet.

Known as the Garifuna, they also maintained a strong sense of family, sexual morality, and belief in the One Creator. They lived along the Caribbean coastline of Central America of Belize and in Honduras.

In Trinidad

Jonas Yunus Mohammed Bath (1783-1838) was a prominent slave in Trinidad. By 1805 at the age fifty-five, he was a freed man and working for the government as a tribunal leader. Mohammed was the religious leader (Imam) of a group of slaves of the Mandingo nation, who were Muslims. In some of his petitions to the British Secretary of State for the colonies he signed it as Sultan Mahmoud II of Alliyant, Chief of the free Negroes of the Mohammedan religion on the Island of Trinidad. Mohammed worked hard to help each one of them to buy their freedom. He and his group systematically bought the freedom of all their members by 1834. Today many of his descendants live in the Port-of-Spain district of St. James.

Yunus petitioned the British three times to send him and his people back to Senegal or Gambia from where they can easily reach their country, it was refused. That forced the Mandingos to settle in Trinidad.

Muhammad Sesei (1788–1838) was another well known leader of the Mandingo Society in Trinidad. Muhammad was determined to return to Africa. He borrowed money from another Muslim, traveled to England with his wife and child, and eventually made it home to his native village Niyani-Maru on the north bend of the Gambia River.

In 1796 Samba Makumba was a Muslim deported to Trinidad as a result of a war. He was from a tribe in Fullah Tauro, where he was an emir. Another Muslim in Trinidad was Mohammadou Maguina, who was of noble birth.

Sylviana Diouf in her book, *Servants of Allah* states that Muslim names found surviving in Trinidad are Mohamed, Abu bakir, Hammadi, Malick, Mohammado, Abdoulie, Salhim, Mohammad, Mohammedu, and Mohammedou.

In Jamaica

Abu Bakir Sadiqi (Edward Donlan) was born in Timbuctoo and was brought up in Jenne. In 1834, in Kingston, Jamaica Abu Bakir wrote his life history. Within his life's story he mentioned five shaykhs (teachers) in his country, Abdulaki Ibn Ali Aga Mahomado Taffosere, Mahomet Wadiwahu, Mahomet Ali Mustapha, Ibrahim Ibn Yusuf, and Ibrahim Ibn Abu Hassan. Abu Bakr Sadiqi's father's name was Hara Musa Sharif. Abu Bakir was captured in a battle. He wrote how his parents were Muslims and about their Islamic life back home. While enslaved he wrote and praised Allah. He wrote, "He who has everything in His power to do as He thinks good, and no man can remove whatever burden He chooses to put on us." And he said, "Nothing shall fall on us except what He shall ordain, He is our Lord, and let all that believe in Him put their trust in Him."

In 1835 special magistrate Robert Madden discovered the presence of a considerable amount of Muslims in Jamaica and recorded the narratives of a selected group. Madden wrote in 1835, that he had a visit one Sunday morning with three Mandingo Negroes, natives of Africa. They all could read and write Arabic. One of them showed him a Koran written from memory. Another was named Benjamin Cockrane "Anna Musa" who was a doctor and lived in Kingston. Anna Musa was enslaved in Tortola, Barbados, and Jamaica. He was the son of a lord in the Carsoe nation.

Muslim names found surviving in Jamaica are Abu Bakr, Harouna, Mohammed, and Musa.

In Haiti

In Haiti from 1753-1757, a Muslim religious leader named MacKandal led numerous raids against the plantation owners. In Surinam, the Bush Blacks were led by Arabi and Zam-Zam. They defeated the Dutch on many occasions and were finally given a treaty and their own territory, near French Guyana.

In Saint- Domingue

In Saint Domingue Pablo Ali (d 1844) was an African-Dominican military leader. During the Haitian Revolution of (1791-1804) Ali crossed the border like many over slaves to serve in the Spanish army of the Domingo for their freedom. In 1811, the Spanish named him first colonel and gave him a gold medal for his service to the crown.

Summary

In closing, I pray that you, the reader have gained some insight into and appreciation of the vast impact and contributions of the African (Black), both non-Muslim and Muslim, who gave so much to the many different societies, communities, and countries the world over. In this humble book we first trace the written biblical history of the African (Black man) dating back to the ancestry of Noah and his descendants who became known as the Semitic, Hamitic, and Japhitic people. We then moved to the descendants of Shem's grandson Eber and his two sons Peleg and Joktan. From Peleg (*Adnan*) and his children came the ancestry of Abraham, Isaac, Jacob, Ismail, and the northern Arabian tribes called the Arabized Arabs (*Al-Arab Al-Musta'ribah*). From Eber's other son Joktan (*Qahtan*) came several of the southern Arabian tribes called the Arabizing Arabs (*Al-Arab Al-Arabiah*).

We then looked at the children of Ham and their descendants, the Hamitic people. Ham's children produced the Akkadians, Abyssinians, Assyrians, Babylonians, Cushities, Canaanities, Egyptians, Hittites, Jebusites, Nubians, and the Phoenicians, just to name a few of the descendants.

We see in Abraham the beginning of the marriage bond or union of the Semitic and Hamitic people. Prophet Abraham (*sa*) married two Hamitic women (*African women*) Hagar the reported mistress, and Ketruah his wife after Sara. Hagar was an African and her son Ismail [Ishmael](*as*) is the ancestor of many Arabian-African tribes. The children of Abraham's second wife Ketruah the African, also produced many Arabian-African tribes. One of the more famous tribes from Ketruah's descendants was the

Midianites, from where Prophet Moses (*sa*) found his wife. The book shows the long relationship and ties between the African and the Arab people, and of the land of Africa and Arabia.

The book pointed out at least ten African heroes/heroines who were leaders before Christ. Cush, Nimrod, Imhotep, Amenophis IV, Nefertiti, Luqman, Queen Sheba, Aesop, Hannibal, and Cleopatra II. It shows that it was an African, Amenophis (Akhenaton) who first preached monotheism.

Many of the great men of color from Islamic heritage who were great military leaders, scholars, writers, poets, explorers, and travelers were highlighted. The book brings the reader up to the 19th century of Islamic leaders and scholars of African heritage. We closed with some of the Muslims found in the Americas who's Islamic faith and light has shined and endured the hardship of an abusive slavery system. They were known for the strength of their Islamic faith and knowledge, some were scholars and religious leaders, while others were military leaders. Some of these Muslims gained their freedom and were businessmen and owners. Many of them could read and write Arabic. Some of them left their own biography, while others left reports of their heroic deeds and works.

Allah (G-d) in the Holy Qur'an reminds the human being that, man was made from dark earth, mud fashioned into shape. Then He Allah (G-d) breathed something of Himself into man. Scientist today now know that the whole human family are descendants from the African. Allah (G-d) in the Holy Qur'an says that He made us as tribes and nations to learn about and from each other not to despise and hate one another.

I hope and pray that we will learn from the lessons in our history and not repeat the same mistakes of the past. I hope that we as a people would remove racism and religious bigotry from our hearts and mind so that we can become a human role model for the entire world. Just as Prophet Joseph (*sa*) was a role model of human kindness and compassion to his brothers and others even after he was thrown into the well and sold into slavery then freed. I would like to end with two quotes from another great man of African heritage of the 20th century, Martin L. King, Jr. who stated that, "Forces that threaten to negate life must be challenged

by courage, which is the power of life to affirm itself in spite of life's ambiguities. This requires the exercise of a creative will that enables us to hew out a stone of hope from a mountain of despair."
"The ultimate measure of a man is not where he stands in the moments of comfort and convenience, but where he stands at times of challenge and controversy."

The African-American Man

W.D. Mohammed, Muhammad Ali,
Thurgood Marshall, Elijah Muhammad,
Martin Luther King Jr.,
Malcolm X (El Hajj Malik Shabazz),
Marcus Garvey, Nobel Drew Ali,
Carter G. Woodson, Paul Lawrence Dunbar,
J.A. Rogers, Jack Johnson, W.E.B. Dubois,
Booker T. Washington, George Washington Carver,
Frederick Douglas, Yarrow Marmood 1807, Abdul Rahman
Ibraham ibn Sori (The Prince Among Slaves, 1828),
Nat Turner, Denmark Vesey, Benjamin Banneker,
Crispus Attucks 1772, Gabriel Prosser,
and David Walker...

And they say I have
no history, no heritage,
no culture, no examples,
no character, and no pride.

Now I wonder why they lie?

For I am the same great African Man
of Yesterday, Today, and Always...

– Amir Muhammad

References

1. Masudul Hasan, *History of Islam*, 1992.

2. Charles Fillmore, *Metaphysical Bible Dictionary,* 1931.

3. *Genesis 11:18-28.*

4. Faruqi & Faruqi, *The Cultural Atlas of Islam*, 1986.

5. Cyril Glasse', *The Concise Encyclopedia of Islam,*
   Harper San Franciso,1989.

6. Rudolph Windosr, *From Babylon to Timbuktu*, 1969. pg.32

7. *Genesis 10:15-18.*

8. J.A. Rogers, *World's Great Men of Color,* Vol. 1, Collier
   Books N.Y., 1947.

9. Kwame Anthony Appiah and Henry Louis Gates, Jr., Africana
   *The Encyclopedia of the African and African American
   Experience*, 1999. Basic Civitas New York

10. Salim Abdul-Khaliq, *The Untold Story of Blacks in Islam*,
    United Brothers & Sisters, 1994.

11. Carter Godwin Woodson, *African Heroes and Heroines*,
    Washington, DC, 1939.

12. Nechemia Levtzion & Randall L. Pouwels, *The History
    of Islam in Africa*, Ohio University Press Ohio 2000.

13. Sylviane A. Diouf, *Servants of Allah; African Muslims
    Enslaved in The Americas*, 1998.

14. Ivan Van Sertima, *African Presence in Early America*,
    Transaction Publishers USA, 1992.

15. Dr. Hakim Quick, *Deeper Roots*, 1996.

16. Amir Muhammad, *Muslims In America Seven Centuries of History,* Amanda Pub.1998.

17. Assad Nimer Busool, *Brave Young Muslim Men*, Al-Huda, Chicago, Illinois1995

18. John Van Seters, *Abraham In History And Tradition,* Yale Press New Haven, CT, 1975.

19. Muhammad Hamidullah, *African (Blacks) Muslims In the Time of the Prophet,* Hyderabad House, Philadelphia.

20. Clyde Ahmad Winters,
    Islam in Early North and South America.

21. Joao Jose Reis, *Slave Rebellion In Brazil,*
    Muslim Uprising of 1835 in Bahia. 1970.

22. P.V. Ramos, *History of the Caribs.*

23. Michael Anthony,
    Historical Dictionary of Trinidad and Tobago.